At the Monster Games

Explorer Challenge

Find out how the monster
gets the fruit …

OXFORD
UNIVERSITY PRESS

Kipper and Lee were reading a story about strange monsters.

"I like the hairy one with big, strong arms!" said Lee.

"What about this one with long legs?" asked Kipper.

"Come and play in our garden games," said Biff.

"Oh no!" Kipper whispered to Lee. "I don't like playing Biff and Chip's garden games. They always win because they're bigger and stronger than me."

"Maybe it will be different today," said Lee. "Let's try!"

The first event was a running race. Wilma was the winner. "Yes!" she said.

Kipper came last and Lee came next-to-last.

"It's not fair," said Kipper. "Wilma has the longest legs!"

Lee and Kipper also came last in the jumping contest ...

... and in the beanbag-throwing contest.

"It's OK," said Biff. "You can't win everything."

Kipper was fed up. "I told you!" he said to Lee.
"I never win *anything*!"

"You were right," agreed Lee. "Let's go inside
and read the monster book."

The others went in to see if Kipper and Lee were OK.
Just then, the key began to glow.

"Come on, you two," said Biff, "let's forget the games
and go on an adventure."

The magic took all the children to a rocky place.

"Where are we?" asked Wilma.

"I have no idea," said Biff. "But look! Something is coming this way!"

Chip squinted. "What is it?" he asked. "Is it an animal?"

The King saw the key in Kipper's hand. "That looks nice," he growled. "Can I see it?"

"Well ..." said Kipper. He did not want to make the monsters cross so he handed the key over.

The King looked closely at the key, and then he popped it into his pocket. "Thanks," he said.

"You can't keep that key," said Wilma.

The crowd of monsters began to growl and grunt crossly.

The King grinned. "Well, it's the Monster Games today," he said. "If any of you can win an event, I'll give back your nice, shiny key!"

"Oh no!" said Kipper.

"That's not fair!" said Biff. "You're bigger than us!"

The first event was a running race.

"You're our fastest runner," Chip said to Wilma.
"You should do this one."

"OK," said Wilma. Then she saw the other runners.
"I don't stand a chance," she said.

"How will we get the key back? We're never going to win anything here!" said Biff.

A monster announced the next event. It was the bouncing race.

The King looked excited. "This is my event," he said.

The King took off his royal robe and got ready to compete.

"His legs look like springs," said Chip. "They are perfect for bouncing!"

Biff stepped forward. "I suppose it's my turn to compete now," she said.

"Wait," said Kipper. "I've got an idea. Can I have a go
at this event?"

"OK," said Biff, uncertainly.

When Kipper joined the monsters at the starting line,
they all laughed at him.

"Excuse me, can you just show me the proper way to bounce?" Kipper asked the King.

The King's grin was enormous. "Like this!" he said.

He began to bounce up and down. He went higher and higher, faster and faster.

The King was bouncing so much that he did not notice when the key fell out of his pocket.

Lee was ready and waiting. He caught the key and began to run.

"Quick!" shouted Kipper.

"Get them!" shouted the King. "They've got my shiny, new key!"

A crowd of monsters rushed towards Kipper and Lee. A big, pink monster tried to grab them, but the children were too quick and small.

Kipper and Lee dodged and ran.

A tall monster with very long legs tried to block them. "Stop!" he yelled.

The boys did not stop – they ran through the monster's legs and kept on going.

They ran towards Biff, Chip and Wilma.

"Go on!" shouted Wilma.

"You're doing brilliantly!" shouted Chip.

The key had started to glow in Lee's hand.

"Quick!" shouted Biff. "Let's go home!"

The King was bouncing towards Lee and Kipper.
"Give me my key back!" he shouted. "It's mine!"
But the key was already taking the children home.
"Sorry," said Biff. "Bad luck!"

Back at home, Chip said, "Wow! That was an exciting adventure!"

Biff was getting something from a drawer. "You two deserve these," she said to Kipper and Lee with a smile.

Biff put medals round Kipper and Lee's necks.

"Well done!" she said. "You dodged those monsters brilliantly!"

"Maybe we should make Monster Dodging an event in our next garden games!" said Chip.

Retell the Story

Look at the pictures and retell the story in your own words.

Look Back, Explorers

Why did Kipper give the magic key to the King?

Why do you think the King grinned when he said "Bad luck!"?

Look at page 24. What other words could you use to describe the big, pink monster?

Who do you think would have won the bouncing contest? Why?

Can you describe how Kipper and Lee got the key from the King?

Did you find out how the monster got the fruit?

Explorer Challenge: using his long tongue (page 21)

What's Next, Explorers?

Now you have read about some monsters that are brilliant at different events, find out about animals that have super speed, super hearing, super strength and lots more ...

Explorer Challenge
for *Animal Superpowers*

Find out what this spider uses the hairs on its legs for ...